P9-DXQ-782

Governing Yourself and Your Family According To What Allāh has Revealed

by Ḥusayn al-'Awāyishah

ISBN 1 898649 67 7

British Library Cataloguing in Publication Data.
A catalogue record for this book is available from the British Library.

© Copyright 2004 by Al-Hidaayah Publishing and Distribution

All rights reserved. No part of this publication may be reproduced in any language, stored in a retrieval system or transmitted in any form or by any means, electronic, mechanical, photocopying, recording or otherwise without the express permission of the copyright owner.

Published: Al-Hidaayah Publishing and Distribution

Distributed by: Al-Hidaayah Publishing and Distribution
P.O. Box 3332
Birmingham
United Kingdom
B10 0UH

Tel: 0121 753 1889
Fax: 0121 753 2422
Website: www.al-hidaayah.co.uk
Email: mail@al-hidaayah.co.uk

Contents

Transliteration Table

Consonants,

ء	'	د	d	ض	ḍ	ك	k
ب	b	ذ	dh	ط	ṭ	ل	l
ت	t	ر	r	ظ	ẓ	م	m
ث	th	ز	z	ع	'	ن	n
ج	j	س	s	غ	gh	ه	h
ح	ḥ	ش	sh	ف	f	و	w
خ	kh	ص	ṣ	ق	q	ي	y

Vowels, diphthongs, etc.

Short:	ـَ	a	ـِ	i	ـُ	u
Long:	ـَا	ā	ـِي	ī	ـُو	ū
diphthongs:			ـَيْ	ay	ـَوْ	aw

Introduction

Indeed, all praise is for Allāh; we praise Him, repent to Him, and seek His forgiveness and help. We seek refuge in Allāh from the evil of our own selves and of our wicked deeds. Whomsoever Allāh guides, none can lead astray; and whomsoever Allāh leads astray, none can guide. And I bear witness that none has the right to be worshipped except Allāh alone, and He has no partner; and I bear witness that our Prophet Muḥammad is His slave and Messenger.

يَٰٓأَيُّهَا ٱلَّذِينَ ءَامَنُوا۟ ٱتَّقُوا۟ ٱللَّهَ حَقَّ تُقَاتِهِۦ وَلَا تَمُوتُنَّ إِلَّا وَأَنتُم
مُّسْلِمُونَ ﴿١٠٢﴾

> O you who believe! Fear Allāh (ﷻ) as He should be feared. And die not except in the state of Islām (as Muslims) with complete submission to Allāh (ﷻ). (Qur'ān 3:102)

يَٰٓأَيُّهَا ٱلنَّاسُ ٱتَّقُوا۟ رَبَّكُمُ ٱلَّذِى خَلَقَكُم مِّن نَّفْسٍ وَٰحِدَةٍ وَخَلَقَ مِنْهَا
زَوْجَهَا وَبَثَّ مِنْهُمَا رِجَالًا كَثِيرًا وَنِسَآءً ۚ وَٱتَّقُوا۟ ٱللَّهَ ٱلَّذِى تَسَآءَلُونَ
بِهِۦ وَٱلْأَرْحَامَ ۚ إِنَّ ٱللَّهَ كَانَ عَلَيْكُمْ رَقِيبًا ﴿١﴾

> O mankind be dutiful to your Lord, who created you from a single person (Ādam), and from him He created his wife, and from them both He created many men and women and fear Allāh (ﷻ) through Whom you demand your mutual (rights), and (do not cut the relations of) the wombs (kinship). Surely, Allāh (ﷻ) is Ever an All Watcher over you. (Qur'ān 4:1)

يَٰٓأَيُّهَا ٱلَّذِينَ ءَامَنُوا۟ ٱتَّقُوا۟ ٱللَّهَ وَقُولُوا۟ قَوْلًا سَدِيدًا ﴿٧٠﴾ يُصْلِحْ
لَكُمْ أَعْمَٰلَكُمْ وَيَغْفِرْ لَكُمْ ذُنُوبَكُمْ ۗ وَمَن يُطِعِ ٱللَّهَ وَرَسُولَهُۥ
فَقَدْ فَازَ فَوْزًا عَظِيمًا ﴿٧١﴾

> O you who believe! Keep your duty to Allāh (ﷻ) and fear Him, and speak (always) the truth. He will direct you to do righteous good deeds and will forgive you your sins. And whosoever obeys Allāh (ﷻ) and His Messenger (ﷺ) he has indeed achieved a great achievement (i.e. he will be saved from the Hell-fire and made to enter Paradise). (Qur'ān 33: 70,71)

Indeed, the most truthful speech is Allāh's Book, and the best guidance is that of Muḥammad (ﷺ). The most evil of affairs are newly invented ones (in the Religion), for every newly invented practice is an innovation (*bid'ah*), every innovation is misguidance, and every misguidance is in the Fire.

Although it is only now that I present this work to the noble reader, it is really one of my earliest of scholarly writings, for I had prepared manuscripts containing its main ideas 23 years ago. The title of this work was mentioned in another book of mine, *The Grave: Its Punishment and Bliss*, which was published approximately 11 years ago. Many brothers then came to me and asked about this work, and some of them even encouraged me, offering their help to publish it; and one such brother, 'Abdullāh al-Sabt, offered to distribute it in Kuwait. But I remained preoccupied for a time in other research projects, even though I came back to this work every once in a while, adding to it here and there. Then finally, I had time to dedicate myself wholly to this work, and Allāh (ﷻ) opened my breast to the idea of completing it. How perfect Allāh is! And all praise and thanks are for Allāh – for his guidance, blessings, and favours.

The subject matter of this work has preoccupied and continues to preoccupy the minds of our Nation's members; yet in spite of this preoccupation, many people lack a correct understanding regarding it. Because the issues that fall under the subject matter of this work are so important, I decided to write this work, through which I hope to make plain the way to live and act according to what Allāh (ﷻ) has revealed.

Contrary to what some may think, this work is relevant not just to leaders, but to every individual as well. Each and every human being is a leader and chief of sorts, for just as a ruler is responsible for the welfare of his state and citizens, each one of us is responsible for his flock – the members of his family and, more importantly, his own self.

Throughout this work, I have tried to defend and support not a group, a *Shaykh*, or the dictates of my desires, but the Muslim Nation and the truth. There would have been no real benefits had I stated in this work that such and such group is right and all others are wrong. Had I stated as much, some people would have been pleased, others would have been saddened, and yet others would have harboured a grudge, but we as a Nation would not have advanced even a single step forward. Our goal is too noble to be wasted on lesser matters.

Today, we as a Nation are afflicted with widespread ignorance. The nations of the world gather against us, just as fellow eaters gather upon their dish. They use every tool at their disposal against us – their wealth, their strength, their technical advancement, their strategy, their deception, and their disbelief. We are in such a state of peril that it is senseless to imagine that a single group among us can put a stop to their constant onslaught.

Our hearts must unite; we must cooperate; we must have correct knowledge; we must work productively; we must be patient; we must make sacrifices; we must give; we must fight our own desires; and we must be sincere.

I ask Allāh (ﷻ) to benefit others through me, to accept [my deeds and this work] from me, to make me a key to goodness and a lock to evil. Verily, He (ﷻ) is upon all things capable.

Ḥusayn Ibn 'Audah al-'Awāyishah

17th of Rabīʿal-Awwal, 1415 H.

"Taking as Lords Rabbis and Monks"

Allāh (ﷻ) said about Jews and Christians:

ٱتَّخَذُوٓا۟ أَحْبَارَهُمْ وَرُهْبَـٰنَهُمْ أَرْبَابًا مِّن دُونِ ٱللَّهِ وَٱلْمَسِيحَ ٱبْنَ مَرْيَمَ وَمَآ أُمِرُوٓا۟ إِلَّا لِيَعْبُدُوٓا۟ إِلَـٰهًا وَٰحِدًا ۖ لَّآ إِلَـٰهَ إِلَّا هُوَ ۚ سُبْحَـٰنَهُۥ عَمَّا يُشْرِكُونَ ﴿٣١﴾

> They (Jews and Christians) took their rabbis and their monks to be their lords besides Allāh, and (they also took as their Lord) Messiah, son of Maryam (Mary), while they were commanded [in the *Taurat* and the *Injīl* to worship none but One *Īlah* (God – Allāh). None has the right to be worshipped but He. Praise and glory be to Him, (far above is He) from having the partners they associate (with Him). (Qur'ān 9:31)

If Allāh (ﷻ) prohibited a matter that their rabbis and priests deemed permissible, Jews and Christians would disobey Allāh and instead follow their rabbis and priests; likewise, if Allāh (ﷻ) permitted a practice that their rabbis and priests forbade, Jews and Christians would follow the latter, deeming that practice to be forbidden. And this is how Christians and Jews took their rabbis and monks to be their lords besides Allāh (ﷻ).

ʿAdī Ibn Ḥātim (رضي الله عنه) said,

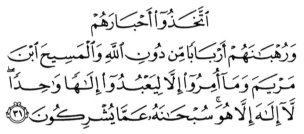

> "I went to the Prophet (ﷺ), and I was [wearing] on my neck a cross made of gold. He (ﷺ) said, 'O ʿAdī! Cast away from your person this idol.' And I heard him recite in Sūrah *Barā'ah* ("The ninth chapter"):

> They (Jews and Christians) took their rabbis and their monks to be their lords besides Allāh.

He (ﷺ) said,

> 'True, they did not worship them (their rabbis and monks), but when they (their rabbis and monks) ruled that something was permissible for them, they (Jews and Christians) would deem that thing to be permissible (even if Allāh forbade that thing upon them). And when they forbade them from something, they would deem that thing to be forbidden (even if Allāh decreed that thing to be lawful).'"[1]

In another narration of the same ḥadīth, it is reported that ʿAdī Ibn Ḥātim (ؓ), who had embraced Christianity before Islām, went to the Prophet (ﷺ), and when he heard the Prophet (ﷺ) recite this verse, he (ؓ) said, "O Messenger of Allāh! Verily, they (Christians and Jews) do not worship them (their rabbis and monks)." The Prophet (ﷺ) said,

> "To the contrary (i.e., they do in fact do so): indeed, they (their rabbis and monks) forbade them from what is lawful, and made lawful for them what is forbidden, and they (Christians and Jews) then followed them (their rabbis and monks). And that is their worship of them."[2]

Allāh (ﷻ) said in the above-mentioned verse that Jews and Christians took their rabbis and monks to be their lords besides Allāh, yet they did not worship them through the act of Prayer, *Ṭawāf* (going around them as people go around the *Kaʿbah*), or any other ostensible act of worship. Therefore, from the verse and from ʿAdī's ḥadīth, it becomes clear that to not rule according to what Allāh (ﷻ) has revealed is a form of worship. In certain situations, then, a person might be worshipping other than Allāh (ﷻ) when he seeks judgement regarding a matter not in Allāh's *Sharīʿah*, but elsewhere.

---

[1] Related by al-Tirmidhī – *Ṣaḥīḥ Sunan al-Tirmidhī* (2471).

[2] This is a *ḥasan* ḥadīth, which our Shaykh – may Allāh have mercy on him – mentioned in *Al-Mustalahāt Al-Arbaʿah Fil-Qur'ān* (Pgs. 18-20).

Ruling According to What Allāh Has Revealed: How?

Simply put, in order to rule according to what Allāh (ﷻ) has revealed, we must deem (both in belief and in deed) forbidden that which Allāh (ﷻ) prohibited, and we must deem lawful that which Allāh (ﷻ) has made lawful.[3] To do that, we must of course know what is lawful and what is prohibited. And we must seek judgement with Allāh (ﷻ) in all matters – Prayer, fasting, *Zakāt*, and *Ḥajj*; marriage banquets and funerals; the way we dress; our food and drink; the affairs of the individual, the family, the society, and the Nation; business matters; the affairs of peace and war; in short, we must seek judgement with Allāh (ﷻ) in all of the affairs of our life.

And let us confidently assert that a person does not really rule according to what Allāh (ﷻ) has revealed if:

- *He ostensibly proclaims the need to establish Islāmic law as a system and way of life, yet he demands a disproportionately large*

---

[3] As for opinions that the people of knowledge arrived at through *Ijtihād* (deriving rulings from revealed sources), it is not correct for one to say that they prohibit what is lawful or make lawful what is prohibited. In fact, a scholar is rewarded for striving to judge based on what he infers from the Qur'ān and Sunnah (of course, only in issues wherein a ruling is not clearly mentioned in the Qur'ān and Sunnah). In an authentically established ḥadīth, the Prophet (ﷺ) said,

> "When a judge issues a correct ruling, he receives two rewards. And when he issues an incorrect ruling, he receives one reward."

sum of money for his daughter's dowry, claiming that he wants to guarantee her future financial independence.

- *He invites others to establish Islāmic law as a system and way of life, yet he submits himself to those customs and traditions of his society – especially for happy occasions – that are contrary to the teachings of Islām.*
- *He propagates the necessity of establishing Islāmic law as a system and way of life, yet when it comes to matters that pertain to funerals, he follows not the guidance of the Prophet (ﷺ), but the customs he inherited from his parents and grandparents.*
- *He calls upon others to establish Islāmic law as a system and way of life, yet he acts contrary to the guidance of the Prophet (ﷺ) in his worship, his deportment, and his dealings.*

Allāh (ﷻ) said:

إِنِ ٱلْحُكْمُ إِلَّا لِلَّهِ ۚ
أَمَرَ أَلَّا تَعْبُدُوٓا۟ إِلَّآ إِيَّاهُ ۚ ذَٰلِكَ ٱلدِّينُ ٱلْقَيِّمُ وَلَٰكِنَّ أَكْثَرَ
ٱلنَّاسِ لَا يَعْلَمُونَ

> The command (or the judgement) is for none but Allāh. He has commanded that you worship none but Him; that is the (true) straight Religion, but most men know not. (Qur'ān 12: 40)

No matter how small or great the matter, its judgement is with Allāh (ﷻ). People act contrary to Allāh's judgement, commands, and prohibitions for a variety of reasons: some because of their tribal or ancestral pride; some because of their love for wealth, a political party, a person, a *Shaykh*, or a group; and some because of other similar reasons.

If we are to rule according to what Allāh (ﷻ) revealed, we must know those revealed texts that make clear the lawful and the forbidden. This of course requires from us that we strive to gain knowledge, gather around scholars, delve into books, and learn from the scholars of the early generations of this Nation. Each person must strive according to his talents and abilities. Some are scholars, so they should teach; and everyone else must learn. And with the exception of scholars who are well grounded in knowledge, people should be careful not to issue legal rulings. They should instead dedicate their time to learning. All of this leads us to:

The Importance of Research and Verification

Without researching and verifying information, one will not be able to rule according to what Allāh (ﷻ) revealed.[4] The Religion is made up of 1) 'Allāh (ﷻ) said,' 2) 'the Messenger of Allāh (ﷺ) said,' and 3) 'the Companions (رضي الله عنهم) said.'

In researching these sources, we must verify that we are not following fabricated reports. The Qur'ān – and all praise is for Allāh – is safe and free from fabrications; nonetheless, we must still research the *Tafsīr* and interpretations of the Qur'ān, making sure that a given interpretation is in agreement with what Allāh (ﷻ) intended. By not taking pains to verify the correctness of an interpretation, people will not be applying that which Allāh (ﷻ) revealed.

As regards the Sunnah, fabrications represent a serious concern. When we say, "The Messenger of Allāh (ﷺ) said," we are speaking about the Religion, and if someone lies upon the Prophet (ﷺ) regarding a ḥadīth, then he has lied upon Allāh (ﷻ). That lie will lead to erroneous legislation in the Religion, erroneous because

[4] Of course I am not saying that everyone should be a scholar, for I am not unaware of the well-known truism: 'If you want to be obeyed, demand only that which can be done.' To become a scholar is a societal obligation: if a sufficient number of people become scholars, then others are absolved of the responsibility of becoming scholars themselves. Nonetheless, those who are not able to study and excel in knowledge must benefit from those who do study and excel in knowledge.

it is legislation that Allāh (ﷻ) did not authorize. Therefore, not researching the authenticity of a ḥadīth results in rulings and judgements that are contrary to what Allāh (ﷻ) has revealed.

True, we despise atheists and communists for deviating from the truth and from Allāh's way; they openly acknowledge their enmity towards Islām and their disbelief in Allāh (ﷻ). But how do we feel about those who deviate from the truth and from Allāh's way, while they claim that they are seeking to please Allāh (ﷻ) and serve Islām!

It is at once odd and sad that some people deride those who follow the methodology of scholarly research and verification. They argue that, "Such exactitude in research prevents people from doing deeds!" But what kind of deeds are they referring to – good or bad? They must be referring to good deeds, since those are the deeds that a Muslim strives to perform. What then is a good deed? How do we know whether a deed is good or bad? When we try to answer these questions, should we follow our mind and our desires, or should we follow revealed texts? Abū Sulaymān al-Dārānī said, "If one is inspired to do a good deed, he should not perform it until he hears about it from an authentic narration. As soon as he does hear about it from an authentic narration, he should do that deed and praise Allāh (ﷻ), thanking Him for the blessing of learning [of a narration] that is in agreement with what was already in his heart."[5]

The good deed or the act of righteousness is mentioned in a number of verses in the Qur'ān; for example, Allāh (ﷻ) said:

فَمَن كَانَ يَرْجُوا۟
لِقَآءَ رَبِّهِۦ فَلْيَعْمَلْ عَمَلًا صَٰلِحًا وَلَا يُشْرِكْ بِعِبَادَةِ رَبِّهِۦٓ أَحَدًۢا

So whoever hopes for the Meeting with his Lord, let him work righteousness and associate none as a partner in the worship of his Lord. (Qur'ān 18: 110)

---

[5] Refer to *Tafsīr Ibn Kathīr*, al-'Ankabūt: 69.

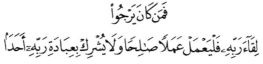

In his *Tafsīr,* Ibn Kathīr said that,

> Let him work righteousness,

refers to deeds that are correct and in agreement with Allāh's *Sharīʿah*; and that,

> And associate none as a partner in the worship of his Lord,

means doing a deed, seeking Allāh's Countenance alone, without associating any partners with Him. These are the two pillars of an accepted deed, for it must be performed sincerely and purely for Allāh (ﷻ), and it must be correct, in accordance with the *Sharīʿah* of the Messenger of Allāh (ﷺ).

A good deed, therefore, is a deed that is harmony with the *Sharīʿah* of Allāh (ﷻ), which means that it is in harmony with the *Sharīʿah* of the Messenger of Allāh (ﷺ). One cannot achieve that harmony or correctness without first going through a process of research, verification, and authentication.

Your goal and preoccupation should not solely be the performance of many deeds, for some or all of those deeds might be contrary to the guidance of the Prophet (ﷺ). Your goal and preoccupation should be the performance of good deeds that are in harmony with the *Sharīʿah* of Allāh (ﷻ).

Ruling by Other than What Allāh has Revealed

Allāh (ﷻ) said:

وَمَن لَّمْ يَحْكُم بِمَآ أَنزَلَ ٱللَّهُ فَأُو۟لَٰٓئِكَ هُمُ ٱلْكَٰفِرُونَ

> And whoever does not judge by what Allāh has revealed, such are the *Kāfirūn*. (Qur'ān 5: 44)[6]

---

[6] In his *Tafsīr*, Al-Baghawī said, "Regarding His saying,

> And whosoever does not judge by what Allāh has revealed, such are the *Kāfirūn*,

and (in the other two verses) *al-Ẓālimūn* and *al-Fāsiqūn*, it is related from al-Barā Ibn ʿĀzib (ﷺ) that these verses are directed at the disbelievers. It has also been said that they are directed at all people. Ibn ʿAbbās (ﷺ) and *Ṭāwus* said, 'It does not refer to the *Kufr* (disbelief) that removes one from the Religion. Rather, if one does it, he is a disbeliever in it (i.e., in the particular ruling he rejects), and he is not like one who disbelieves in Allāh and the Last Day.' ʿAtā said, 'It is a lesser *Kufr*, a lesser *Ẓulm*, and a lesser *Fisq*.' ʿIkrimah said, 'What it means is that if a person does not rule by what Allāh has revealed, doing so because he disbelieves [in what Allāh has revealed], then he has disbelieved. And if one accepts what Allāh has revealed but does not rule by it, then he is a *Ẓālim* (evildoer) and a *Fāsiq* (rebellious, disobedient transgressor).' When ʿAbdul-ʿAzīz Ibn Yaḥyā al-Kannānī was asked about these three verses, he said, 'They apply not only to portions of what Allāh (ﷻ) has revealed, but to everything that Allāh (ﷻ) has revealed. Whoever does not rule according to everything that Allāh (ﷻ) has revealed is a *Kāfir* (disbeliever), a *Ẓālim* (evildoer), and a *Fāsiq* (rebellious, disobedient, transgressor). As for he who rules according>

to what Allāh (ﷻ) has revealed in matters that pertain to *Tawḥīd* (Islāmic Monotheism) and to abandoning *Shirk* (associating partners with Allāh in worship), but who does not rule by certain legislations that Allāh (ﷻ) has revealed, then the ruling of these verses do not necessarily apply to him.' The scholars have said: 'All of this applies to a person who knowingly and purposefully rejects a clear judgement from Allāh, and not to a person who is unaware of that judgement or errs in his interpretation.'"

In *Zād al-Masīr*, Ibn al-Jawzī said, "Who are these verses revealed about? Scholars disagree about the answer to this question, there being five distinct views:

1) They were revealed specifically about the Jews. This view is related from ʿUbayd Ibn ʿAbdullāh from Ibn ʿAbbās (رضي الله عنه). And Qatādah also expressed this view.

2) They were revealed about Muslims. Saʿīd Ibn Jubayr related a view from Ibn ʿAbbās (رضي الله عنه) that more or less conveys this meaning.

3) The implications of these verses are general, applying to both Jews and the members of this Nation. Ibn Masʿūd (رضي الله عنه), al-Ḥasan, al-Nakhaʿī, and al-Ṣiddī all expressed this view.

4) They were revealed about Jews and Christians. Abū Mujliz stated this view.

5) Of the three verses, the first one is revealed about the Muslims; the second, about the Jews; and the third, about the Christians. Al-Shaʿbī asserted this opinion.

And as for the intended meaning of *Kufr* (disbelief) in the first verse, there are two views:

1) It refers to disbelief (*Kufr*) in Allāh (ﷻ).

2) It refers to disbelief (*Kufr*) in the particular judgement that is not applied; hence it is not the disbelief (*Kufr*) that removes one from the Religion.

The following is the correct view [in regards to all of the previous issues]: Whoever does not rule by what Allāh has revealed, disbelieving in it (in what Allāh has revealed), though he knows that Allāh revealed it (the particular judgement or command or prohibition that he is not applying) – and this is what the Jews did – then he is a *Kāfir* (a disbeliever). And whoever does not rule by what Allāh revealed, not from disbelief, but from an inclination to follow one's desires, then he is a *Ẓālim* (evildoer) and a *Fāsiq* (rebellious, disobedient transgressor)." >

Ibn Kathīr said in his *Tafsīr*, "Regarding the verse,

> And whosoever does not judge by what Allāh has revealed, such are the *Kāfirūn*,

Ibn Al-Ṣiddī said, 'If a person does not rule by what has been revealed, and if he abstains from doing so on purpose...and with full knowledge, then he is from the disbelievers. Concerning the same verse, 'Alī Ibn Abī Ṭalhah reported that Ibn 'Abbās (رضي الله عنه) said, 'If a person rejects what Allāh (ﷻ) has revealed, then he has disbelieved. But if a person accepts what Allāh (ﷻ) has revealed [though he does not apply it], then he is a *Ẓālim* and a *Fāsiq*.' Ibn Jarīr, who related this last narration, chose the view that the verse refers to the People of the Book (Jews and Christians) or to those who reject the judgement of Allāh that is revealed in the Book (the Qur'ān). 'Abdur-Razzāq related from al-Thaurī, from Zakariyyah, from Al-Sha'bī that,

> Whosoever does not judge by what Allāh has revealed,

is directed at Muslims. Ibn Jarīr related another narration from Al-Sha'bī in which he said that,

> And whosoever does not judge by what Allāh has revealed, such are the *Kāfirūn*,

is for the Muslims; that,

> And whosoever does not judge by that which Allāh has revealed, such are the *Ẓālimūn* (polytheists and wrong-doers),

is for the Jews; and that,

> And whosoever does not judge by what Allāh has revealed (then) such (people) are the *Fāsiqūn* [disobedient ones].,

is for the Christians. 'Abdur-Razzāq related from Mu'ammar, from Ibn Ṭāwus, from his Father, who said, 'Ibn 'Abbās (رضي الله عنه) was asked about Allāh's saying:

> And whosoever does not judge...,

and he said: Not judging [by what Allāh revealed] is disbelief.' Ibn Ṭāwus said, 'A person who does this is not like (i.e., is of a lesser degree>

than) the one who disbelieves in Allāh, His Angels, His Books, and His Messengers.' Al-Thaurī related from Ibn Jurayj that 'Atā said, 'It is *Kufr* (disbelief) of a lesser degree than [the well-known] *Kufr* (disbelief), *Ẓulm* of a lesser degree than [the well-known] *Ẓulm*, and *Fisq* of a lesser degree than [the well-known] *Ẓulm*.' Regarding the first verse,

> And whosoever does not judge by what Allāh has revealed, such are the *Kāfirūn*,

Wakī' related from Sa'īd al-Makkī that Ṭāwus said, 'It is not the *Kufr* (disbelief) that takes one outside of the Religion.' And regarding the same verse, Ibn Abī Hātim related this saying from Ibn 'Abbās (ﷺ): 'It is not the *Kufr* (disbelief) that you are thinking about.' Al-Ḥākim related the previous narration from Sufyān Ibn 'Uyaynah, and he said, 'It is authentic and fulfills the conditions of al-Bukhārī and Muslim, though they did not relate it.'"

In Rūḥul-Ma'ānī, al-Alūsī said, "They are perhaps given three descriptions (*Kufr*, *Ẓulm*, and *Fisq*) that are each appropriate to an aspect of their action. So because they refuse [to rule by what Allāh has revealed], they are described as being *Kāfirūn* (disbelievers); because they rule incorrectly, they are described as being *Ẓālimūn* (evildoers); and because they have abandoned the truth, they are described as being *Fāsiqūn* (rebellious, disobedient transgressors). Or perhaps they are described based on the stages of their refusal to rule [by what Allāh has revealed]. At times, their refusal involves *Kufr*; and at other times, it involves *Ẓulm* or *Fisq*."

Abū Ḥumayd and others related that al-Sha'bī said, "Of the three verses in [Sūrah] *Al-Mā'idah*, the first is for this Nation, the second is for the Jews, and the third is for the Christians." This suggests that the believers are in a worse situation than the Jews and Christians; however, it has been said that, when *Kufr* is ascribed to the believers, it is to show a degree of severity; and that, when the words *Fisq* and *Ẓulm* are ascribed to the disbelievers, it is to indicate the insolence and rebelliousness of their disbelief. This is supported by a narration in which Ibn 'Abbās (ﷺ) said about the *Kufr* that is mentioned in the first of the three verses, "It is not the *Kufr* that you are thinking about; it is not the *Kufr* that takes one outside of the Religion; rather, it is *Kufr* of a lesser degree than [that] *Kufr*." (Ibn al-Mundhir, al-Ḥākim, and al-Bayhaqī, in his *Sunan*, related this narration, and >

al-Ḥākim declared it to be authentic.)...Some eminent scholars from the later generations said that *Kufr* (disbelief) is the intended meaning of the last two verses as well; they take the view that complete and utter *Fisq* and *Zulm* are intended (*Kufr* must certainly then be involved at that high level of *Fisq* and *Zulm*). Al-Ḥākim, ʿAbdur-Razzāq, and Ibn Jarīr related the following narration from Ḥudhayfah (※), and al-Ḥākim declared it to be authentic: 'The three [aforementioned] verses were mentioned in the presence of Ḥudhayfah (※), and a man then said, 'These [verses] are referring to the Children of Israel.' Ḥudhayfah (※) said, 'What wonderful brothers the Children of Israel are to you, if you are to have everything that is sweet, and they everything that is bitter! Nay! By Allāh, you will follow their path to the measurement of a shoelace (an expression meaning, 'you will follow them very closely and precisely.').' Perhaps this means that Ḥudhayfah (※) was inclined to the view that these verses apply to everyone; or perhaps, as it has been said, that he was inclined to the view that they are addressed specifically to Muslims. The former possibility is related from ʿAlī Ibn al-Ḥusayn (※), except that he added in his narration, '*Kufr* (disbelief) that is not like the *Kufr* of *Shirk* (associating partners with Allāh in worship), *Fisq* that is not like the *Fisq* (evildoing) of *Shirk*, and *Zulm* that is not like the *Zulm* of *Shirk*.'"

And finally, al-Shinqītī – may Allāh have mercy on him – said in *Al-Aḍwā Al-Bayān*: "Regarding the topic at hand, in order for one to have a correct understanding it is crucial to know that the words *Kufr*, *Zulm*, and *Fisq* are each used in the *Sharīʿah* to mean 'sin' sometimes, and '*Kufr* (disblief)' – which takes one outside of the Religion – at other times. So if one does not rule by what Allāh has revealed, with the intention of opposing the Messengers and nullifying Allāh's commands, then his *Fisq*, *Zulm*, and *Kufr* are all that *Kufr* which removes one from the Religion. And if one does not rule by what Allāh has revealed, though he believes that he is perpetrating a forbidden and wicked deed, then his *Kufr*, his *Zulm*, and his *Fisq* do not remove him from the Religion...The context of [these three verses in] the Qurʾān indicates that first verse is about the Muslims, the second is about the Jews, and the third is about the Christians; nonetheless, we must consider the generality of the words' implications, and not the specific reasons that occasioned them (so for these verses, even if one of the verses is about the Jews, we must take heed as well).... [And Allāh (※) knows best]."

And Allāh (ﷻ) said:

وَمَن
لَّمْ يَحْكُم بِمَآ أَنزَلَ ٱللَّهُ فَأُو۟لَـٰٓئِكَ هُمُ ٱلظَّـٰلِمُونَ

And whosoever does not judge by that which Allāh has revealed, such are the *Zālimūn* (polytheists and wrong-doers). (Qur'ān 5: 45)

And Allāh (ﷻ) said:

وَمَن لَّمْ يَحْكُم بِمَآ أَنزَلَ ٱللَّهُ فَأُو۟لَـٰٓئِكَ هُمُ ٱلْفَـٰسِقُونَ

And whosoever does not judge by what Allāh has revealed (then) such (people) are the *Fāsiqūn* [the rebellious, disobedient ones]. (Qur'ān 5: 47)

And Allāh (ﷻ) said:

أَلَمْ تَرَ إِلَى ٱلَّذِينَ يَزْعُمُونَ أَنَّهُمْ ءَامَنُوا۟ بِمَآ أُنزِلَ إِلَيْكَ
وَمَآ أُنزِلَ مِن قَبْلِكَ يُرِيدُونَ أَن يَتَحَاكَمُوٓا۟ إِلَى ٱلطَّـٰغُوتِ
وَقَدْ أُمِرُوٓا۟ أَن يَكْفُرُوا۟ بِهِۦ وَيُرِيدُ ٱلشَّيْطَـٰنُ أَن يُضِلَّهُمْ
ضَلَـٰلًۢا بَعِيدًا ﴿٦٠﴾

Have you seen those (hypocrites) who claim that they believe in that which has been sent down to you, and that which was sent down before you, and they wish to go for judgement (in their disputes) to the *Ṭāghūt* (false judges, etc.) while they have been ordered to reject them. But *Shayṭān* (Satan) wishes to lead them far astray. (Qur'ān 4: 60)

And Allāh (ﷻ) said:

فَلَا وَرَبِّكَ لَا يُؤْمِنُونَ
حَتَّىٰ يُحَكِّمُوكَ فِيمَا شَجَرَ بَيْنَهُمْ ثُمَّ لَا يَجِدُوا۟
فِىٓ أَنفُسِهِمْ حَرَجًا مِّمَّا قَضَيْتَ وَيُسَلِّمُوا۟ تَسْلِيمًا ﴿٦٥﴾

But no, by your Lord, they can have no Faith, until they make you (O Muḥammad (ﷺ)) judge in all disputes between them, and find in themselves no resistance against your decisions, and accept (them) with full submission. (Qur'ān 4: 65)

'Urwah (⁂) related the incident that occasioned the revelation of this last verse. He (⁂) said, "Al-Zubayr disputed with a man from the Anṣār over a stream of water from Al-Hirrah (A well-known place in al-Madīnah).[7] The Prophet (⁂) said (in his judgement),

> 'Water [your land], O Zubayr, then let the water flow to your neighbour (Zubayr's land was situated closer to the water source, so this was a most just judgement, which also took into consideration the needs of Zubayr's Anṣārī neighbour).' The Anṣārī said, 'O Messenger of Allāh! It is (i.e., you have ruled so) because he is your cousin from your aunt.' The Prophet's face coloured [in anger], and he then said, 'Water [your land], O Zubayr! Then hold the water back until it returns to the source of the garden, and then let the water flow to your neighbour.' Before the Anṣārī angered him, the Prophet (⁂) gave a solution that was for the benefit of both parties; but then [after the Anṣārī angered him] the Prophet (⁂) gave Zubayr (⁂) his full right in a clear ruling (it was his full right since his land was situated closest to the water source). Al-Zubayr (⁂) said, 'I think that it was specifically this incident, and no other, that occasioned the revealing of these verses:
>
> But no, by your Lord, they can have no Faith, until they make you (O Muḥammad (⁂)) judge in all disputes between them.'"[8]

---

[7] In the Arabic language, Al-Harrah refers to a land that abounds with black stones that are decayed to the extent that it seems as if they were burned by fire.

[8] Related by al-Bukhārī (4585) and Muslim (2357).

Judging by What Allāh (ﷻ) has Revealed in All Matters

The revealed texts that order us to rule by what Allāh (ﷻ) has revealed are general, in that they embrace every single thing, matter, and situation. The Messenger of Allāh (ﷺ) said,

> "Whosoever from you sees evil, then let him change it with his hand; if he is not able to do so, then with his tongue; and if he is not able to do so, then with his heart. And that (the last level, changing evil with one's heart) is the weakest [level of] *Īmān* (Faith)."[9]

The Muslim must remove the evil he sees, and in doing so, he must proceed according to the three aforementioned levels or stages. And he cannot be selective, removing only certain evils; according to his ability, he must remove every evil he sees. The perpetration of wicked deeds and innovations, lawful matters being prohibited, and prohibited matters being made lawful – these are all evil matters that the Muslim must strive to remove. Simply because a person calls upon others to rule by what Allāh (ﷻ) revealed on a societal level, does not mean that he is excused from the duty of removing the aforementioned evils.

When a Nation fosters deeds of obedience to Allāh (ﷻ) among its members, it is a Nation that will achieve happiness in both worlds – the happiness of *Khilafah* on the earth, and the happiness of Paradise in the Hereafter. Allāh (ﷻ) said:

---

[9] Related by Muslim (49).

إِنَّ ٱللَّهَ لَا يُغَيِّرُ مَا بِقَوْمٍ حَتَّىٰ يُغَيِّرُوا۟ مَا بِأَنفُسِهِمْ

> Verily! Allāh will not change the good condition of a people as long as they do not change their state of goodness themselves (by committing sins and by being ungrateful and disobedient to Allāh). (Qur'ān 13: 11)

The Prophet (ﷺ) said,

> "When you make ʿĪnā business transactions (one that involves usury), when you take the tails of cows (an expression that refers to becoming preoccupied with worldly matters), when you are contented with farming, and when you forsake *Jihād*, then Allāh will set humiliation over you, and He will not remove it until you return to your Religion."[10]

In this ḥadīth, the Messenger of Allāh (ﷺ) mentioned the causes of humiliation and defeat – conducting ʿ*Īnā* transactions and being preoccupied with farming (and worldly affairs in general) instead of with *Jihād* in the way of Allāh (ﷻ). These are the causes of humiliation and defeat, but what is the way to safety? We know the disease, but what is the cure? Are we to continue conducting ʿ*Īnā* transactions [and all other business transactions that Allāh forbade]? Are we to continue to remain preoccupied with farming [and worldly endeavours] while we forsake *Jihād* in the way of Allāh? Shall we remain ignorant about our Religion? If a person tells someone not to conduct ʿ*Īnā* transactions, should he be told that he is needlessly quibbling about a minor detail and that he lacks 'depth' in his understanding? But then is not our constant state of humiliation the result of ʿ*Īnā* transactions and all forbidden business transactions (such as usury)?

As long as we continue to do business in ways that Allāh (ﷻ) has forbidden, we will not be able to remove the cover of humiliation

---

[10] Related by Abū Dāwūd (*Ṣaḥīḥ Sunan Abū Dāwūd* – 2956); by al-Bayhaqī in *Sunan al-Kubrā*; and by al-Ṭabarānī and others, as has been mentioned by our Shaykh – may Allāh have mercy on him – in *Al-Silsilat al-Ṣaḥīḥah* (11).

that envelopes us. The cure to our woes is clear: "...until you return to your Religion."

In explaining *Rabbāniyyūn* from the verse,

كُونُوا رَبَّـٰنِيِّـۧنَ

Be you *Rabbāniyyūn*. (Qur'ān 3: 79),

Ibn 'Abbās (رضي الله عنه) said, "Forbearing scholars who have an understanding [of the Religion]." And it is said that *al-Rabbānī* (singular of *Rabbāniyyūn*) is a person who raises and teaches people in clear issues of knowledge before [teaching them] detailed or difficult issues of knowledge.[11]

The goal of a person who teaches *'Aqīdah* (beliefs), *Tawḥīd* (Islāmic Monotheism), and *al-Asmā Wa l-Ṣifāt* (Allāh's perfect names and attributes) should be to benefit his student by rectifying his beliefs, with a complete realization that he is laying the foundations of the building that is Islāmic Law (ruling by what Allāh has revealed). And when one prays, he should pray with sincerity, without thinking that his deed is irrelevant to the goal

---

[11] Bukhārī mentioned this *Mu'allaqan*, but with a wording that evinces a sense of sureness (*Kitāb al-'Ilm, Bāb al-'Ilm Qablal-Qawl Wa l-'Amal*). Al-Ḥāfiẓ said in *al-Fatḥ* (1/161): "The saying [of Ibn 'Abbās (رضي الله عنه)] is related with a connected, *ḥasan* chain by Ibn Abī 'Āsim. Al-Khaṭīb related it with another chain that is also *ḥasan*. Ibn 'Abbās (رضي الله عنه) interpreted *al-Rabbānī* to mean a person who is wise and has a deep understanding of the Religion (a *Faqīh*). Ibrāhīm al-Ḥarbī related that Ibn Mas'ūd (رضي الله عنه) concurred with Ibn 'Abbās's interpretation of the term *al-Rabbānī*. Al-Asma'ī and al-Ismā'īlī stated that *al-Rabbānī* is closely linked to the word *al-Rabb* (the Lord), because a person who is *Rabbānī* is one who, in his knowledge and deeds, seeks and strives to apply what *al-Rabb* (the Lord – Allāh) commanded him with. Tha'lab said, 'Scholars are called *Rabbāniyyūn* because they undertake the task of preserving and spreading knowledge.' Hence there is disagreement over whether the term has its roots in the word '*al-Rabb*' or in the word '*Tarbiyyah*' (to raise and educate)..... And Ibn al-'Ārābī said, 'A scholar is not called *Rabbānī* until he is a scholar who teaches and applies [what he knows].'"

of establishing Allāh's rule (His *Sharīʿah*); rather this and other good deeds are individual bricks that combine to complete the structure. Similarly, one should realize that, by closely following the Sunnah of the Prophet (ﷺ), one is taking a step forward towards establishing Allāh's *Sharīʿah* on earth.

In this regard, we should not be blind to the fact that many verses of the Qur'ān were revealed even before the establishment of the Islāmic State; in those verses, Allāh (ﷻ) ordered the Messenger of Allāh (ﷺ) to warn [others about the Day of Judgement], to stand at night to pray, and to do other similar good deeds. And to be sure, Allāh (ﷻ) is most capable of allowing the formation of an Islāmic state before all of that; thus we should realize that there is a decreed way in which matters progress – preliminaries, if you will, in the path of establishing Allāh's rule and *Sharīʿah* in the land.

Complete Obedience and Submission

By reflecting on the story of Ibrāhīm (عليه السلام), of when, in answer to Allāh's command, he left his wife and child in a land that was bereft of people and water, one should learn many important lessons. In answer to Allāh's command, Ibrāhīm (عليه السلام) left his wife and child in a dry, barren land; he didn't argue by saying, 'What is the wisdom and benefit in doing this?' Instead, he hastened to answer and obey his Lord's command.

Ibn ʿAbbās (رضي الله عنه) related this ḥadīth: "When certain [known] events took place between Ibrāhīm (عليه السلام) and his wife (Sarah), he left with Ismāʿīl (عليه السلام) [and Ḥājar], and with them was an old canteen that contained water. The mother of Ismāʿīl began to drink from the canteen, and her milk would then flow abundantly for her child. When he (Ibrāhīm) reached Makkah, he placed her under a large tree. Then Ibrāhīm returned to his family, but [at first] she followed him until they reached Kaddā, when she called out from behind him, 'O Ibrāhīm, to whom do you leave us?' He (عليه السلام) said, 'To Allāh (i.e. to His care).' She said, 'I am pleased with Allāh.' She returned and began to drink from [her] canteen, and her milk would then flow abundantly for her child. When there was no more water, she said, 'If I go and look [around], perhaps I will find someone.' So she went, climbed al-Ṣafā (a well-known mountain in Makkah), and looked again and again in the hope of seeing someone. But she didn't see anyone. Then when she reached the valley, she moved briskly until she reached al-Marwah (another well-known mountain in Makkah). She made a number of circuits in this fashion (between al-Ṣafā and al-Marwā), and she then said, 'I should go and see what he (the child) did (i.e., I should go and see what happened to him).' She went and looked, only to find him upon a state in which it seemed as if he was breathing rapidly due to the approach of death. She was much disquieted, and she said, 'If I go and look, maybe I will find someone.' So she went and climbed al-Ṣafā, and she looked again and again, without finding anyone; she continued [to look] until she completed seven [circuits between al-Ṣafā and al-Marwā]. Then she said, 'I should go and see what he has done (referring to her child),' but suddenly she heard a voice. She then said, 'Help, if you have any goodness with you [to offer].' It was Jibrīl (ﷺ), and he did this with his heel, and he struck his heel on the ground. Water then gushed out, and the mother of Ismāʿīl was amazed." Ibn ʿAbbās (رضي الله عنه) said, "She began to rush, and ʿAbul-Qāsim (i.e., the Prophet (ﷺ)) said, 'Had she left it (allowed it to gush forth without rushing), the water would have flowed on the surface of the earth.' She began to drink from the water, and her milk then flowed abundantly for her child. Then people from Jurhum passed by from the middle of the valley, at which point they came across a bird. It was as if they disbelieved what they saw (Makkah was barren and the presence of a bird signified that there was a water source nearby), and they said, 'A bird is only found over [or near] water.' So they sent their messenger, who went and looked. They were really near water (the Zamzam source), so he returned and informed them about it. They went to her (to Ḥājar) and said, 'O mother of Ismāʿīl! Do you give us permission to be with you – or to live with you?' [They did settle there] and when her son reached puberty, he married one of their women (one of the women of Jurhum). An idea then occurred to Ibrāhīm (عليه السلام), and so he said to his wife (Sarah), 'I am indeed going to check on those that I left behind [in Makkah].' He (عليه السلام) went, extended greetings of peace [to Ismāʿīl's wife], and said, 'Where is Ismāʿīl?' Ismāʿīl's wife said, 'He has gone hunting.' He said, 'Say to him when he comes: Change the threshold of your door.' When Ismāʿīl (عليه السلام) returned, she informed him of what happened [and of Ibrāhīm's message]. He (عليه السلام) said, 'That is you (i.e., Ibrāhīm (عليه السلام) was referring to you when he said, 'Change the threshold of your door.'), so return to your family (i.e., you are divorced).' Then [later on] Ibrāhīm had an idea, and so he said to his wife (Sarah), 'I am indeed going to check on those I left behind.' He came and said, 'Where is Ismā'īl?' Ismā'īl's wife (for he had married again) said, 'He has gone hunting. Will you not remain to eat and drink?' He (ﷺ) said, 'What is your food and drink?' She said, 'Our food is meat, and our drink is water.' He said, 'O Allāh, bless them in their food and drink.'" At this point in the narration, Ibn 'Abbās (رضي الله عنه) said, 'Abul-Qāsim (i.e., the Prophet (ﷺ)) said, 'Blessing through the supplication of Ibrāhīm (i.e., through that supplication, there are blessings in Makkah).' Then [later on] Ibrāhīm had an idea, so he said to his wife (Sarah), 'I am indeed going to check on those whom I left [in Makkah].' He then came and [this time he] met Ismā'īl (عليه السلام) behind the Zamzam [well], where he was mending his arrows. Ibrāhīm (عليه السلام) said, 'O Ismā'īl! Indeed, your Lord ordered me to build a house for Him.' Ismā'īl (عليه السلام) said, 'Obey your Lord.' He (عليه السلام) said, 'Indeed, He has commanded me that you should help me to do so.' Ismā'īl (عليه السلام) said, 'Then I will do so,' – or those were his approximate words. They then stood. Ibrāhīm (عليه السلام) started to build while Ismā'īl (عليه السلام) handed him the stones, and they were both saying,

رَبَّنَا تَقَبَّلْ مِنَّآ إِنَّكَ أَنتَ ٱلسَّمِيعُ ٱلْعَلِيمُ

> "Our Lord! Accept (this service) from us. Verily! You are the All-Hearer, the All-Knower." (Qur'ān 2: 127)."[12]

Ibrāhīm's wife asked him, "To whom are you leaving us?" And in certain of al-Bukhārī's narrations, she repeated this question or plea over and over again, yet throughout, he did not turn around to answer her; finally, she said, "Did Allāh order you to do this?" He (عليه السلام) said, "Yes." She said, "Then He will not allow us to waste away (or perish)." In another narration, she said, "I am pleased with Allāh (i.e., with His decree and with being placed in His care)." She did not, however, say, "There are priorities. Instead of

---

[12] Related by al-Bukhārī (3365).

leaving us in this barren desert, you should take us with you, for we can then help you in calling others to the way of Allāh."

If we know that a command is from Allāh (ﷻ), we must only do as the mother of Ismā'il did: answer and obey. Being pleased with Allāh's decree, she began to move briskly from al-Ṣafā to al-Marwā, now hoping to find water, and now fearing for her son who was on the verge of dying.

Some who have weak faith might say, "This was the calamity of near death for the child! What did this experience benefit him, his father, or his mother!" Such people do not appreciate the *Jihād* and patience and sacrifices of Ibrāhīm (عليه السلام) and his family; instead, such people uphold a purely worldly view – the very view that has effectively struck down our Nation.

From a realistic and sensible point of view, let us ask, what were the fruits of Ibrāhīm and his wife's obedience to Allāh (ﷻ)? They are fruits that were reaped not just by Ibrāhīm (عليه السلام), his wife, and his child; rather they are fruits that every Islāmic Monotheist on the face of the earth has reaped and will continue to reap until the coming of the Hour.

Muslims come to Makkah in throngs from both the east and the west. They are happy and contented because they are making circuits between al-Ṣafā and al-Marwā, in the same place that the mother of Ismā'il performed the same circuits. They come from far-off lands in order to train themselves to obey Allāh's commandments. As they move briskly between the two said mountains, they reflect on how the mother of Ismā'il raced back and forth in a state of pain and sadness, placing obedience to her Lord before all else.

Then, by the permission of Allāh, the water of Zamzam gushed forth, water that contains a cure to diseases and sickness and that is blessed and excellent. To this very day, Muslims are eager to drink as much as they can from that very same water and to transport it to their homelands, no matter the distance and the hardships involved.

And Ibrāhīm (عليه السلام) built the Inviolable House. The rewards of praying there are many times greater than the rewards of praying elsewhere. People also achieve the rewards of performing *Ṭawāf* around the Ka'bah, and their supplications are answered. These are the benefits of answering and obeying Allāh's commands, benefits that extend beyond those who obeyed to those that came after them.

Then let us too be obedient to our Lord, even if doing so apparently involves some fatigue, hardship – or even death. Let us forbid ourselves from disobedience and transgression. Will we not then consider and reflect?

A similar lesson can be found in the story of how Mūsa's mother, by the command of Allāh (سبحانه وتعالى), threw her child into a river.

وَأَوْحَيْنَآ إِلَىٰٓ أُمِّ مُوسَىٰٓ
أَنْ أَرْضِعِيهِ ۖ فَإِذَا خِفْتِ عَلَيْهِ فَأَلْقِيهِ فِى ٱلْيَمِّ وَلَا تَخَافِى
وَلَا تَحْزَنِىٓ ۖ إِنَّا رَآدُّوهُ إِلَيْكِ وَجَاعِلُوهُ مِنَ ٱلْمُرْسَلِينَ ٧

> And We inspired the mother of Mūsa (Moses), (saying): "Suckle him (Mūsa), but when you fear for him, then cast him into the river and fear not, nor grieve. Verily! We shall bring him back to you, and shall make him one of (Our) Messengers." (Qur'ān 28: 7)

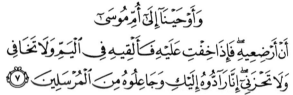

When Allāh (سبحانه وتعالى) commanded Mūsa's mother to throw her child into the river, she could only obey. If she had been seen by someone who knew not of her circumstances, her action would have appeared to have been precipitated by a fit of madness, for how would she or Mūsa (عليه السلام) benefit from her casting him into a river? Yet in the end, the benefits of her action were beyond what any person could have imagined. Because she obeyed Allāh's command, her child was safely returned to her. She was saved from sadness, and instead became pleased, knowing that Allāh's promise is true. And her son, Mūsa (ﷺ), became from "The Messengers of Strong Will."[13]

When you are told to do something, do not ask, "What is the benefit of doing this?" But instead say, "Did Allāh order me to do this? Did His Messenger (ﷺ) order me to do this? Is there any established proof from revelation regarding this matter?" After all, our happiness lies in the obedience of Allāh (ﷻ), even though some acts of obedience seemingly involve a certain degree of fatigue or hardship. Conversely, utter and true misery lies in turning away from Allāh's commands, even if doing so seemingly offers a life of comfort and happiness in this world.

One does well to reflect on the reason why stories like these are related in the Qur'ān and Sunnah. They are not related to entertain, but rather to serve as a reminder and to strengthen the hearts of the believers.

وَكُلًّا نَّقُصُّ عَلَيْكَ مِنْ أَنۢبَآءِ ٱلرُّسُلِ مَا نُثَبِّتُ بِهِۦ فُؤَادَكَ

> And all that We relate to you (O Muḥammad (ﷺ)) of the news of the Messengers is in order that We may make strong and firm your heart thereby. (Qur'ān 11: 120)

[13] Refer to the Qur'ān: 46:35

Priorities?[14]

First, however great the importance or stature of a thing, it is one part of the whole or a branch of the foundation; the whole is composed of parts and the foundation branches out. Even the *Shahādah* (Testimony of Faith: "None has the right to be worshipped but Allāh") is a part of the *Shahādatayn* (The Two Testimonies of Faith: "None has the right to be worshipped but Allāh, and Muḥammad is the Messenger of Allāh"). I will now further explain these principles.

The realization of a Muslim society that is ruled by the Muslim *Khalīfah* is the ardent desire of every Muslim of sound mind. Yet a person who merely desires for that to occur wishes to live in a huge castle that has yet to be built. First, the ground on which the

---

[14] To be sure, the principle which says that, "The more important matter should be given precedence over the important matter," is true and must neither be discarded nor denied. However, we don't want this principle to be wrongly used as a weapon against those who strive to do good deeds, for that will only lead to the abandonment of both the more important matter and the important matter, of both primary matters and secondary matters. All that will then remain will be talk and slogans. Furthermore, if there are obstacles preventing us from applying more important matters, should we consequently abandon important matters that we can apply? Indeed, to apply important matters will pave the way for us, so that we can then apply more important matters at a later time.

Our main concern should be to always fear Allāh (ﷻ) as much as we are able to. Then, if our situation becomes constricted to the point that we can apply one matter only, we must give precedence to the more important matter over the important matter, to the obligatory deed over the voluntary one.

castle is to be built must be dug deep; the foundations must be made firm and strong. When the earth is being dug, can a person of sound mind say, "Why are you digging downward when you should be building upward? You are delaying the building of the castle?" He is not sane, for he wants the whole (or the end result) without the development of the parts. Seeing quantities of steel in one place, quantities of bricks and cement in another place, and quantities of wood in yet another place, he laments: "What will this steel and this wood and these bricks do to help realize the building of a castle?" But if we gather these scattered parts along with even other parts, we can build the large castle and realize our hopes and wishes.

Such is the case of 'insignificant details' and 'secondary matters.' If you were to look at every deed by itself, you might be tempted to disparage it and say, "How will this contribute to building a Muslim society and establishing Allāh's rule on earth?"

By attending a lesson in *Tawḥīd* (Islāmic Monotheism), giving a small amount of charity, performing two units of prayer, doing a generous deed, ordering others to do good, and forbidding them from performing evil or innovation, you might be tempted to say, "These are scattered parts, none of which can destroy the foundations of an ignorant society or establish the structure of an Islāmic society." But if you combine these parts, you will realize that they make up the whole and that the whole is composed of them. The above-mentioned deeds and others as well are parts of the building that is the Muslim society.

How easy it is to speak about the comprehensiveness and completion of the Religion of Islām! Of course we must not disparage those who speak with understanding and knowledge about the comprehensiveness of Islām, or those who point out the importance of establishing Allāh's rule (His *Sharīʿah*), for this is the goal of every Muslim. Nonetheless, speaking about the comprehensiveness of Islām and the importance of establishing Allāh's rule (His *Sharīʿah*) must not hinder us from consistently performing those deeds that we are able to perform. I say that it is easy to speak about the comprehensiveness of Islām because the ignorant person or child can speak about it before even the adult or the wise scholar. This is because merely speaking about the building of a huge castle does not bring it into existence, and merely talking about the comprehensiveness of Islām does not establish a country for its application. So let us embrace all aspects and parts of the Religion – knowledge, action, sincerity, patience, struggle, and firmness.

We must also be careful to remember that parts of a whole are not independent; they are all related to the whole just as branches are not separate entities but are instead attached to the base or foundation.

It is true to say that if we were to have a truly Muslim society that is governed by Allāh's rule (His *Sharīʿah*) and that is led by a noble *Khalīfah*, the various parts of that society – families and individuals – would prosper, with a sound Islāmic awareness in *Tawḥīd* (Islāmic Monotheism), *Fiqh* (Jurisprudence), and good manners; they would be good in their dealings and in preserving acts of obedience and worship. Both men and women would adorn themselves with Islāmic clothing; they would consume lawful food and drink; they would strive to avoid mixing, and they would fulfil all other religious duties.

But if there is no Muslim *Khalīfah*, can we not realize all or at least some of the matters I mentioned above? Indeed it is the responsibility of every shepherd, or if you will, every lesser ruler, to educate and train himself, his children, and all whom he is able to influence.

I take refuge in Allāh from saying words here that down play the importance of the Muslim *Khalīfah*. To be sure, his presence has a tremendous influence on changing the state of society. But here I am talking about a person who says or who, through his actions, effectively says that certain aspects of the Religion should be forsaken since there is no Muslim ruler. He claims all the while that those aspects of the Religion keep one preoccupied away from establishing Allāh's *Sharīʿah*.

True, there are certain things that cannot be accomplished without a Muslim ruler, and this is something that we must not overlook. Yet there are also matters that cannot be accomplished without one struggling with his own self, and this occurs on the level of the individual, of the ruled, of the citizen.

Every Person is a Ruler and a Chief

Abū Hurayrah (🙏) reported that the Messenger of Allāh (ﷺ) said,

> "Every person from the children of Ādam is a chief: A man is chief over his family, and a woman is the chief of her house."[15]

In another ḥadīth, the Prophet (ﷺ) said,

> "Every one of you is a shepherd, and every one of you is responsible for his flock. The *Imām* is a shepherd, and he is responsible for his congregation. A man is shepherd among his family, and he is responsible for his flock (his family). A woman is shepherd in her husband's home, and she is responsible for her flock. A servant is shepherd over the wealth of his owner, and he is responsible for his flock…"[16]

So regardless of whether we have a Muslim ruler or not, every single one of us is a shepherd, a leader, a chief, a commander, a guardian in his home – with tremendous responsibilities that he must fulfil.

As is related in the following ḥadīth, Islām is a number of handgrips (things that are held and adhered to, here referring to the various legislations of Islām):

---

[15] Related by Ibn al-Sinnī in *Deeds of the Day and Night* and by others. It is an authentic ḥadīth, which our *Shaykh* – may Allāh have mercy on him – related in *al-Ṣaḥīḥah* (2041) and said, "This is an authentic chain, and it fulfills the conditions of Muslim."

[16] Related by al-Bukhārī (893) and Muslim (1829).

"The handgrips (i.e., the teachings and legislations of Islām) of Islām will be undone one handgrip at a time. Every time one handgrip is undone, people will hang on to the one that follows it. The first of them to be undone is *al-Ḥukm* (Islāmic rule)[17] and the last of them is the Prayer."[18]

Therefore, Islām is made up of parts that hold together; the most important of those parts is Islāmic rule, which comprises Prayer, *Zakāt*, *Ḥajj*, etc. Just because a Muslim is busy calling upon society to establish Allāh's *Sharīʿah* as a way of life and as a constitution of a country, he is not excused from the duty of applying Allāh's *Sharīʿah* in his life, among his family, and among all whom he is able to influence.

This is important to understand because some people who, for instance, call upon others to correct their beliefs and raise their level of understanding are accused of frustrating the efforts of others who are trying to establish Allāh's *Sharīʿah* in the land.

In another example, you might find people who get frustrated when they are told to straighten their lines for Prayer; they might say, for example, "This is not what we should preoccupy ourselves with these days." But if one were to reflect on the Prophet's command regarding this practice, one would come to an opposite conclusion. The Messenger of Allāh (ﷺ) said,

"Straighten [your lines] and do not differ (in your bodies, by not being lined up in straight rows); otherwise your hearts will differ."[19]

Al-Nuʿmān Ibn Bashīr (؇) reported that the Prophet (ﷺ) said,

---

[17] This proves the importance of the Muslim *Khalīfah* and of Islāmic rule. Without Islāmic rule, the other handgrips are easily undone. Nonetheless, to rebuild requires striving to establish Allāh's *Sharīʿah*, but before that happens we need to train the individual, the family, and society.

[18] Related by Aḥmad; by Ibn Ḥibbān, in his *Ṣaḥīḥ*; and by al-Ḥākim, who ruled that it is authentic. Refer to *Ṣaḥīḥ al-Targhīb Wa l-Tarhīb* (569).

[19] Related by Muslim (432).

> "You will indeed straighten your lines, or Allāh will indeed cause your faces to differ (i.e., He will cause your hearts to differ, and He will cause enmity and hatred to spread among you)."[20]

In another narration, al-Nūʿmān Ibn Bashīr (رضي الله عنه) said,

> "The Messenger of Allāh (ﷺ) turned towards the people with his face, and he (ﷺ) said, 'Establish your rows (by straightening them and filling in the gaps) – he (ﷺ) repeated this three times. By Allāh, you will establish your rows or Allāh will cause your hearts to differ among yourselves."[21]

The Prophet (ﷺ) plainly stated that not straightening the rows in Prayer leads to discord among the hearts of people. They are therefore wrong who say that speaking about the importance of straightening the rows divides the hearts of people and diverts them from the more important teachings of the Religion.

Discord among the hearts of people then leads to failure, destruction, and a dissipation of strength. Allāh (تعالى) said:

وَلَا تَنَٰزَعُواْ فَتَفۡشَلُواْ وَتَذۡهَبَ رِيحُكُمۡ

> And do not dispute (with one another) lest you lose courage and your strength depart. (Qur'ān 8: 46)

And the Messenger of Allāh (ﷺ) said,

> "Do not differ among yourselves, for indeed, those who came before you differed among themselves, and they were then destroyed."[22]

If we combine the meanings of the above-mentioned *aḥādīth* and verse, this is the meaning we are left with:

"Straighten your rows, and do not differ (neither in your

---

[20] Related by al-Bukhārī (717) and Muslim (436).

[21] Related by Abū Dāwūd (*Ṣaḥīḥ Sunan Abī Dāwūd* – 616). And Ibn Ḥibbān related it in his *Ṣaḥīḥ*.

[22] Related by al-Bukhārī (2410).

bodies when you are lined up for Prayer nor in your hearts); otherwise, you will be destroyed, you will fail, your strength will depart, and your enemies will defeat you."

One who thinks that, if we are to establish Allāh's *Sharī'ah* on earth, we must ignore straightening the rows in Prayer and other similar issues in the Religion, is like a person who thinks that Prayer is more important than fasting and all else, and so he reproaches those who talk about the importance of fasting or the prohibition of usury-based dealings. They are both wrong, for obligatory deeds in the Religion are as many as they are varied. And the Muslim is required to perform them to the utmost of his ability.

Therefore, there is no just reason to say that some duties clash with other duties. Performing *Jihād* in the way of Allāh is obligatory; inviting others to the way of Allāh is obligatory; waging war on false beliefs is obligatory; fighting the spread of backbiting and slander is obligatory; being dutiful to one's parents is obligatory; straightening the rows is obligatory; a Muslim is responsible, according to his ability, for all of these duties.

When one says that there are priorities – the more important duty and the important duty – he is speaking the truth. However, we need to know about priorities not in order to forsake our duties, but in order to coordinate and classify our duties and in order to race to perform good deeds.

For every matter that is important, there is another that is even more important. This even applies to the two testimonies of faith, for "None has the right to be worshipped but Allāh," is more important than, "Muḥammad is the Messenger of Allāh." Yet the presence of what is more important does not play down or nullify what is important. It is only when a situation becomes difficult and constricted, when one is able to apply only one of two or more matters that he should give priority to the most important matter. This is akin to the way we sometimes – when we are short on time, for instance – give precedence to the obligatory deed over the voluntary one.

When circumstances are not straitened, which is the rule and not the exception, then we must strive, according to our ability, to apply both the more important and the simply important matter. We proceed in this manner in light of Allāh's saying,

لَا يُكَلِّفُ ٱللَّهُ نَفْسًا إِلَّا وُسْعَهَا

> Allāh burdens not a person beyond his scope. (Qur'ān 2: 286),

and in light of the Prophet's saying,

> "Whosoever from you sees evil, then let him change it with his hand; if he is not able to, then with his tongue; and if he is not able to, then with his heart. And this (changing evil with one's heart, by at least sincerely hating it) is the weakest [level] of *al-Īmān* (Faith)."[23]

And we must not forget the jurisprudential principle: "It is not permissible to delay clarifying [the ruling in an issue] until after its needed time." Let us suppose that you hear a person mentioning a fabricated ḥadīth; will you delay telling him about his mistake until after Allāh's *Sharīʿah* is applied as a way of life and as a constitution of a country? Are you hoping that you can then inform him that a number of years ago he mentioned a fabricated ḥadīth? What guarantee do you have that both of you will be alive when Islām has a country? What guarantee do you have that you will remember all of the wrongs you did not redress in years gone by, or all of the good deeds that you did not enjoin others to perform? When you see someone performing an evil deed, will you postpone reproaching him until the Islāmic country is established? Or will you apply the aforementioned ḥadīth:

> "Whosoever from you sees evil..."

'Evil' in the ḥadīth is expressed as an indefinite noun, which indicates that the ḥadīth is referring to evil that is both great and small.

---

[23] Related by Muslim (49).

The methodology of the Companions (ﷺ) in performing *Da'wah* is epitomized in the story of 'Umar Ibn al-Khaṭṭāb's death. Here is part of a narration that gives an account of his death: "...Then he ('Umar (ﷺ)) was carried to his house. We too went with him. [So sad was everyone that] it was as if the people had never been afflicted with a calamity before that day. A person said, 'It is okay (i.e., he will recover from his wounds),' while another said, 'I fear for him.' *Nabīẓ* (a kind of drink; basically it is water in which dates are soaked, so as to make a sweet drink) was brought to him, and he drank it, but it then came out from his insides. Then milk was brought to him (ﷺ), and he drank it, but it came out from his wound. And so they knew that he was dying. We entered upon him, and the people came [as well]. They began to praise him. A young man came and said, 'Rejoice, O Leader of The Believers, with the glad tidings of Allāh for you, for being a Companion of the Messenger of Allāh (ﷺ), and for your service to Islām from the early days – of which you know – and then you governed and were just. Then (now) [you achieved] martyrdom.' 'Umar (ﷺ) said, 'I wish that that was *Kafāf* (i.e., that I come out even) – neither against me nor for me.' When he (the young man) turned away, his lower garment was touching the ground.' 'Umar (ﷺ) said, 'Send the lad back to me.' He (ﷺ) said, 'O son of my brother! Raise your garment, for doing so will make your garment last longer and will signify that you fear your Lord to a greater degree.'[24]

'Umar (ﷺ) ordered the young man to raise his garment and to shorten the length of his lower garment. Was he eating a meal consisting of fruits and sweets when he advised the young man? No, he advised him and called him to apply a particular teaching of Islām while he was in the most dangerous of situations. He advised the young man at a time when the Muslims were

---

[24] Related by al-Bukhārī: 3700. The commentary that follows is from my book, *"The Story of 'Umar Ibn al-Khaṭṭāb's Murder."*

experiencing a deep sense of grief, when he himself was facing death and bidding farewell to life. The Muslims were preoccupied about the issue of the *Khilāfah* (leadership), and they were anxious about ʿUmar's health. So extreme was their grief that ʿAmrun Ibn Maymūn described it thus: "It was as if the people had never been afflicted with a calamity before that day." ʿUmar (رضي الله عنه) advised the boy to raise his garment [above his ankles] at a time when thirteen men from the Companions were stabbed, and of those thirteen, seven died.

How then can a person say: "This is not the time to forbid people from allowing their garments to fall below the level of their ankles. Now is not the time to warn against innovations. Now is not the time to encourage people to adhere to authentic *aḥādīth* and to forsake weak ones. Now is not the time to speak about such matters."

If you pride yourself in being from the same Nation as ʿUmar (رضي الله عنه), then follow his way. His way was to highlight the importance of obeying the commands of Allāh (عز وجل) and His Messenger (ﷺ). He (رضي الله عنه) did not divide the Religion and say that certain matters are of prime importance and must be followed while other matters, though they may be compulsory in terms of application, represent the outer shell of Islām and hence are not so important. Rather, he (رضي الله عنه) obeyed Allāh (عز وجل) in every single matter that he had knowledge about, regardless of whether that knowledge was acquired from the Book of Allāh (عز وجل) or from the Sunnah of the Messenger of Allāh (ﷺ).

How many teachings do we forsake because we feel that they are secondary matters, which divert us from *Jihād* and from establishing Allāh's *Sharīʿah* on earth? Where is the *Jihād* that we have performed and where is the Islāmic country that we have realized? We have neither performed *Jihād* nor established Allāh's *Sharīʿah* on earth; nor have we avoided innovations and forbidden deeds. I do not see any conflict between our various goals. Let us make correct preparation for *Jihād* in the way of Allāh (عز وجل), and let us strive to establish Allāh's rule (His *Sharīʿah*) in the land. And let us also forbid one another from innovations and evil deeds, while calling upon one another to perform good deeds. In what way are these duties at variance with one another?

A Lack of Understanding

It is because important issues are unclear in the minds of a rather large number of Muslims that some people say, "These are insignificant details; these are differences that we do not want to delve into; there are more important issues." As a result of not knowing Allāh's ruling in certain issues, many such people unintentionally make light of Allāh's commands.

On one occasion, immediately after Prayer, a noble brother and caller from an Islāmic organization said to me, "*Taqabbalallāh* [May Allāh accept (this deed from us)], but perhaps you will say that this is an innovation (i.e., that saying, '*Taqabbalallāh*,' after Prayer is an innovation)."[25] After discussing the matter with him, I finally said, "I want you to give me a single example of an innovation in the Religion. You may choose any example you want." By Allāh, he was not able to come up with anything, despite the fact that he had went through higher [Islāmic] education and that he was highly involved in calling others to the way of Allāh (ﷻ). Why was this so with him? It is because he did not have a clear understanding of true scholarly methodology [in learning]. And there are many people that are like this noble brother.

Their problem is that, in arguing that an actual innovation is not an innovation, they rely on general revealed texts. For

---

[25] By way of induction from legislative principles, [we know that] this phrase is permissible if it is not adhered to always (as if it is a part of the Prayer); this ruling has been clearly expressed by some of the people of knowledge. However, to say it always (as if it is a part of the Prayer or a practice from the Sunnah) requires proof, since the rule in matters of worship is [that a deed] is forbidden unless a proof establishes it.

example, they might say that it is permissible for the Caller to Prayer (*Muaddhin*) to send prayers upon the Prophet (ﷺ) in a loud voice, immediately upon performing the *Adhān* (call to Prayer) – thus making it a part of the *Adhān*. The general revealed text that they rely on in this issue is the saying of Allāh (ﷻ):

إِنَّ ٱللَّهَ وَمَلَٰٓئِكَتَهُۥ يُصَلُّونَ عَلَى ٱلنَّبِيِّ

> Allāh sends His *Ṣalāt* (Graces, Honours, Blessings, Mercy, etc.) on the Prophet (Muḥammad (ﷺ)) and also His angels too (ask Allāh to bless and forgive him). (Qur'ān 33: 56)

In another example, they might say that, based on the following verse, it is permissible for people to remember Allāh (ﷻ) in unison with others, in a loud voice, and on a continual basis.

فَٱذْكُرُونِيٓ أَذْكُرْكُمْ

> Therefore remember Me (by praying, glorifying, etc.). I will remember you. (Qur'ān 2: 152)[26]

Regarding the same issue, they might cite this saying of the Prophet (ﷺ):

> "Upon you is *Al-Jamā'ah* (the main body of Muslims), for the wolf only eats the solitary, distant sheep."[27]

---

[26] They also cite this ḥadīth that is related by Muslim (384):

> "When you hear the *Muaddhin* (the Caller to Prayer), then say as he says; then send prayers upon me…"

In no way does this ḥadīth support their view. First, this ḥadīth is addressed not to the *Muaddhin* but to those who hear him. Second, the Prophet (ﷺ) said, "…then say as he says; then send prayers upon me…" Had the *Muaddhin* sent Prayers upon the Prophet (ﷺ) [out loud after the call to Prayer], the Prophet (ﷺ) would not have said, "Then send prayers upon me," for his saying, "Say as he says," would then have sufficed.

[27] This ḥadīth is *ḥasan*, and it is related by Aḥmad, Abū Dāwūd, al-Nisā'ī, Ibn Khuzaymah, Ibn Ḥibbān (these last two related it in their *Ṣaḥīḥ* compilations), and al-Ḥākim. Refer to *Nuṣūṣ Hadīthiyyah* (pg. 13) and *Ṣaḥīḥ al-Targhīb wa l-Tarhīb* (pg. 427).

It is certainly forbidden to reject these verses and *aḥādīth*; what we rightly reject, however, is how people incorrectly infer views from them in the above-mentioned issues and in other issues as well.

Let us suppose that a man prays five units (*Rak̲a῾āt*) for the ῾*Īsha* Prayer instead of the prescribed four units. Would a person who generally condones innovations say that his action is legislated or even permissible? If he says, "No," and he has no choice but to say, "No," then we would say to him, "Well, Prayer has a very high and important status in the Religion, a fact that is established in many verses of the Qur'ān and sayings of the Prophet (ﷺ). Each time a person performs prostration to Allāh (ﷻ), he draws nearer to Allāh (ﷻ), for Allāh (ﷻ) said:

وَٱسْجُدْ وَٱقْتَرِب

...Fall prostrate and draw near to Allāh! (Qur'ān 96: 19).

And the Prophet (ﷺ) said, 'It is when he is prostrating that the slave is closest to his Lord, so supplicate much and often [when you are prostrating].'"[28] If he then says, "But it is not related from the Messenger of Allāh (ﷺ) that he prayed five units for the obligatory portion of the ῾*Īsha* Prayer," we would then say to him, "This is the argument we wanted to hear from you. In the above-mentioned issues, has anything specific been related from the Prophet (ﷺ)?"

Is it related from the Messenger of Allāh (ﷺ) that he ordered one of his Callers to Prayer to send prayers upon him out loud, immediately upon completing the *Adhān* (call to Prayer)? Or is that related from the Companions? Yes, it is true that our Lord (ﷻ) said:

إِنَّ ٱللَّهَ وَمَلَٰٓئِكَتَهُۥ يُصَلُّونَ عَلَى ٱلنَّبِيِّ

Allāh sends His *Ṣalāt* (Graces, Honours, Blessings, Mercy, etc.) on the Prophet (Muḥammad (ﷺ)) and also His angels too (ask Allāh to bless and forgive him). (Qur'ān 33: 56)

---

[28] Related by Muslim (482).

This verse was known to the Messenger of Allāh (ﷺ) before any other human being, for it was revealed to him, and it is the truth from our Lord (ﷻ). Yet the Messenger of Allāh (ﷺ) ordered neither Bilāl (رضي الله عنه) nor any other *Muaddhin* (Caller to Prayer) to send prayers upon him out loud and immediately after the *Adhān* (call to Prayer). And as far as I know, this practice is not related from any of the Companions (رضي الله عنهم). This, despite the fact that the *Adhān* was performed on innumerable occasions, so that had anyone during the Prophet's time applied the said practice, news thereof would have reached us.

By now you should perceive why the *Dāʿī* (caller to Islām) who prayed beside me was not able to give even one example of an innovation. He, like others of his ilk, relies on revealed texts that impart general rulings. Even had he mentioned an innovation, I could have – in keeping with his false methodology – mentioned a general proof to legitimize that innovation, just as he does to legitimize other innovations. This is why we need a basic yet solid foundation in our understanding of *bidʿah* (innovations). If we agree that innovations exist, we must then ask how it is that we can distinguish between innovation and Sunnah. In my view, we can only answer this question by always demanding for a revealed text which specifically establishes or warrants a given act of worship. So if a person want to perform the *Adhān* (call to Prayer) for the Funeral Prayer or for the ʿĪd Prayer, and if he mentions the virtues of the *Adhān* to further his claim, we will say to him, "But is there anything related from the Prophet (ﷺ) or from his Companions (رضي الله عنهم) regarding them performing the *Adhān* for the Funeral Prayer or for ʿĪd Prayer?"

Similarly, if someone wants to perform the *Sunan al-Rawātib* prayers in congregation, based on the ḥadīth, "Upon you is the *Jamāʿah* (congregation or main body of Muslims)," we will say to him, "But is that practice specifically related from the Prophet (ﷺ) or from his Companions (رضي الله عنهم)?"

If we don't follow this methodology in distinguishing between Sunnah and *bid'ah*, every act of worship will become legitimized, without the need for evidence or proof, and *bid'ah* would then no longer exist. In a narration that is related by Abi al-Salt, a man wrote to 'Umar Ibn 'Abdul-'Azīz (⁕), asking him about Divine Preordainment. 'Umar (⁕) wrote back this response: "As for what follows, I advise you to fear Allāh, to be neither excessive (or perhaps harsh, or perhaps excessive in the sense of adding to the Religion) nor negligent (or perhaps negligent in the sense of taking away from the Religion) in His commands, to follow the Sunnah of His Prophet (⁕), and to forsake what the innovators have innovated (i.e., new matters that they have introduced into the Religion). The Sunnah of the Prophet (⁕) is established, and you have been sufficed [through the authentic Sunnah] from having to carry the weight of innovations (and Allāh has completed the Religion for His slaves). It is incumbent upon you to adhere to the Sunnah, for indeed – by the permission of Allāh – it is a protection for you. Then know that people have not introduced any innovation except that a lesson or proof has come before it to establish that it is indeed an innovation [and an act of misguidance]. Verily, the one who has established the Sunnah knew what is contrary to it (so he surely mentioned the ruling for what is contrary to the Sunnah, namely, *bid'ah*), in terms of error, mistakes, foolishness, and excessiveness. So be pleased – for yourself – with what the people (i.e., the pious predecessors) were pleased with."[29] In summary, for every particular act of worship we need a specific proof, because innovations are deemed legitimate based on revealed texts that are general in their implications. 'Umar Ibn 'Abdul-'Azīz's saying confirms this rule. And success lies with Allāh (⁕).

---

[29] Related by Abū Dāwūd (*Ṣaḥīḥ Sunan Abī Dāwūd*: 3856).

Knowing Allāh (سبحانه وتعالى)

If a person believes that Allāh is the All-Hearing, the All-Seeing, the All-Knowing, and that there is nothing like unto Him, then he is more qualified than others to know that the judgement of the All-Hearing is not like the judgement of those whose hearing is weaker than His; that the judgement of the All-Seeing is not like the judgement of those whose sight is weaker than His; that the ruling of the All-Knowing is not like the ruling of those who have less knowledge than He has; and that, just as there is nothing like unto Him in His Self, His Names, and His Attributes, there is no judgement and rule like His judgement and rule, and no legislation like His legislation. It is a mistake, therefore, to separate one category of *Tawḥīd* from another, or to distance and separate some revealed texts from other revealed texts.

Ibn ʿUmar (رضي الله عنهما) reported that the Messenger of Allāh (ﷺ) said, "Verily, the Nations before you were not destroyed until they committed something similar to this – using parts of the Qur'ān against other parts [of the Qur'ān]. As for what is *Ḥalāl* (permissible), make it *Ḥalāl*; and as for what is *Ḥarām* (forbidden), then make it *Ḥarām*. And as for what is *Mutashābih* (what is unclear to people or what is clear only to the people of knowledge), then believe in it."[30]

---

[30] An authentic ḥadīth that al-Ṭabarānī related in *al-Kabīr* and that others related as well. It is from *Ṣaḥīḥ al-Jāmiʿ* (1334). And refer to *al-Ṣaḥīḥah* (1522).

The Ill Effects of Sins

Ibn 'Umar (ﷺ) related that the Messenger of Allāh (ﷺ) said,

> "O group of *Muhājirīn*! When you are put to trial by five matters...and I seek refuge in Allāh from you being around when they come to pass:
>
> (1) No abomination (wickedness, such as fornication) appears among a people until they perform it out in the open, except that such plague and suffering will spread among them as have never existed among their predecessors who have departed.
>
> (2) They (people) will not decrease in measure and in the balance (i.e., they will not cheat others when trading in measure or weight) except that they will be afflicted with drought, with harsh conditions, and with the tyranny of the ruler against them.
>
> (3) They will not refuse to give *Zakāt* on their wealth, except that they will be refused (or denied) rain from the sky, and had it not been for the beasts, it would not have rained.
>
> (4) They will not break [their] covenant with Allāh and with His Messenger, except that Allāh will empower over them an enemy from other than them, [an enemy] that will take some of what they have in their hands. And
>
> (5) as long as their leaders do not rule by Allāh's Book, and [as long as they] choose from what Allāh has revealed [taking only that which they like], then Allāh will make their suffering occur at the hands of one another (i.e., they will fight one another)."[31]

---

[31] Related by Ibn Mājah, Abū Nu'aym in *al-Ḥilyah*, and others. It is an authentic ḥadīth, and our *Shaykh* – may Allāh have mercy on him – related it in *al-Ṣaḥīḥah* (106).

In this ḥadīth, the Prophet (ﷺ) said,

> "They (people) will not decrease in measure and in the balance (i.e., they will not cheat others when trading in measure or weight) except that they will be afflicted with drought, with harsh conditions, and with the tyranny of the ruler against them."

This proves that sins result in tyranny at the hands of the ruler and in judgement by other than what Allāh (ﷻ) has revealed.

The Importance of Knowledge

How are we to establish Allāh's *Sharīʿah* on earth without knowledge? Upon which *Madh-hab* will we bring that about? To establish Allāh's *Sharīʿah* on earth, we most definitely need scholars and students of knowledge; we need scholarly research; we need to be diligent and patient; and we need to work hard and raise our level of faith through training and education.

To every noble brother who strives to achieve goodness and to fight evil and deviation, I say: May Allāh bless you in your efforts, but do not forget to carry the sword of knowledge. How are false creeds defeated? By Allāh, you will not be able to bring an end to false creeds without knowledge. How many people have debated with adherents of false creeds, only to be defeated because of a paucity of knowledge! Suppose you are able to convince someone that his beliefs are false; do you have the knowledge to then teach him correct beliefs and the right methodology?

In teaching others, one can of course rely on nothing better than the Qur'ān, the Sunnah, and the guidance of our pious predecessors. To teach people based on these sources requires scholars, students of knowledge, reliable books, and the ability to discern between the authentic and the unauthentic.

represent the outer shell."[33] Yet you will find that he doesn't even apply what he considers to be the 'core issues' of Islām. He only argues as he does in order to escape from having to apply certain teachings of Islām.

My advice to a person who criticizes others who are trying to their utmost to apply the Religion is to ask himself these questions: "What have I contributed to myself, to my family, and to the Muslims? What have I put forward in terms of good deeds? And what have I done in terms of bad deeds?" 'Abdullāh Ibn Mas'ūd (ﷺ) related that the Prophet (ﷺ) said,

> "He will not enter Paradise who has an atom's weight (or the weight of a tiny ant) of pride in his heart."

A man said, "Verily, a man loves for his garment to be nice and for his shoes to be nice." The Prophet (ﷺ) said,

> "Verily, Allāh is Beautiful, and He loves beauty. Pride is to reject the truth and to look down upon and disparage people."[34]

And the Prophet (ﷺ) said,

> "Three [matters] destroy, and three [matters] save [a person from destruction]. The three that destroy are stinginess that is complied with, desire that is followed, and a person having a high opinion of his own self. The three that save [one from destruction] are fear of Allāh, both in secret and out in the open; moderation in poverty and in richness; justness in anger and in contentment."[35]

---

[33] By Allāh, I am amazed at this naming which leads to the disparagement of certain aspects of the Religion. He spoke well who gave the answer: "Let us suppose that you have coined a correct expression, but shouldn't you remember that the core is always protected by the outer shell."

[34] Related by Muslim (91).

[35] By dint of all of its chains being considered together, this ḥadīth is *ḥasan*. For a detailed discussion of this ḥadīth, refer to *al-Ṣaḥīḥah* (1802).

Observe how having a high opinion of one's own self is a cause of destruction, and how justness in both anger and contentment saves one [from destruction]. And so we ask Allāh (ﷻ) to bless us with justness in all of our affairs, in our judgement of groups and their messages, regardless of whether we are angry or content. And we ask Allāh (ﷻ) to help us against the desires of our souls. Indeed, He (ﷻ) is upon all things capable.

Finally, I want to remind myself and my brothers about these important *aḥādīth*:

Musʿab Ibn Saʿad related from his Father (رضي الله عنه) that it appeared to him that he had merit (perhaps because of his strength, bravery, and other similar qualities) over those that were below him from the Companions of the Messenger of Allāh (ﷺ), and so the Prophet (ﷺ) said,

> "Indeed, Allāh only helps this Nation through its weak ones – through their supplication, their prayer, and their sincerity."[36]

In another ḥadīth, the Prophet (ﷺ) said,

> "Ardently seek out the weak ones for me (or, 'bring close to me the weak ones,' or, 'fulfil the rights of the weak ones, ask how they are doing, and be generous to them'), for you are provided for and aided only because of them (or, 'it is only through them that you are provided for and helped')."[37]

---

[36] Related by al-Nisā'ī and others. It is also found in *Ṣaḥīḥ al-Bukhārī* and other compilations, but without the mention of 'sincerity.' Al-Mundharī mentioned this in *al-Targhīb wa l-Tarhīb* (1/54). It is an authentic ḥadīth, and it is discussed at length in *al-Ṣaḥīḥah* (2/423).

[37] Related by Abū Dāwūd, al-Nisā'ī, al-Tirmidhī, and others. It is an authentic ḥadīth, and it is discussed at length in *al-Ṣaḥīḥah* (779).

Conclusion

Here ends what I have been able to write on this topic, and all praise belongs to Allāh, for His help and guidance. And I ask Him (ﷻ) for guidance and correctness in all matters. I ask Him to inspire me to apply that which I have written about and to accept this work from me. And I ask Him to benefit Muslim men and women in all parts of the earth through this book. Indeed, He is All-Hearing, All-Knowing.